NATIONAL GEOGRAPHIC

Sea and Land
Animals

Sarah Dawson

Animals that live in the sea may seem very different from animals that live on the land.

But they are not always so different.

Some animals have sharp teeth to bite their food.

A shark has sharp teeth.
It uses its sharp teeth to bite into its food.
A shark lives in the sea.

A lion has sharp teeth.
It uses its sharp teeth to bite into its food.
A lion lives on the land.

5

Some animals have claws to tear their food.

A lobster has claws.
It uses its claws to tear its food.
A lobster lives in the sea.

A bear has claws.
It uses its claws to tear its food.
A bear lives on the land.

Some animals have fur to keep them warm.

A sea otter has fur.
Its fur helps keep it warm in cold water.
A sea otter lives in the sea.

A rabbit has fur.
Its fur helps keep it warm in cold weather.
A rabbit lives on the land.

Some animals have hard shells to protect their bodies.

A crab has a hard shell.
Its hard shell protects its soft body.
A crab lives in the sea.

A tortoise has a hard shell.
Its hard shell protects its soft body.
A tortoise lives on the land.

Some animals have sharp spines to protect themselves from enemies.

A sea urchin has sharp spines.
Its spines help protect it from enemies.
A sea urchin lives in the sea.

A hedgehog has sharp spines.
Its spines help protect it from enemies.
A hedgehog lives on the land.

Some animals have stripes that hide them from enemies.

A clown fish has stripes.
Its stripes help it to hide from enemies.
A clown fish lives in the sea.

A tiger has stripes.
Its stripes help it to hide from enemies.
A tiger lives on the land.

15

Index